Pablo Picasso

Published by Roaring Brook Press
Roaring Brook Press is a division of Holtzbrinck Publishing Holdings Limited Partnership
120 Broadway, New York, NY 10271
mackids.com

Library of Congress Control Number: 2018955958
ISBN 978-1-250-16898-6

Our books may be purchased in bulk for promotional, educational, or business use. Please contact your local bookseller or the Macmillan Corporate and Premium Sales Department at (800) 221-7945 ext. 5442 or by email at MacmillanSpecialMarkets@macmillan.com.

First published in France in 2015 by Quelle Histoire, Paris
First U.S. edition, 2019

Text: Patricia Crété
Translation: Catherine Nolan
Illustrations: Bruno Wennagel, Mathieu Ferret

Printed in China by RR Donnelley Asia Printing Solutions Ltd., Dongguan City, Guangdong Province
10 9 8 7 6 5 4 3 2 1

Pablo Picasso

Roaring Brook Press
New York

Budding Painter

Pablo Ruiz Picasso was born in Málaga, Spain, on October 25, 1881. His father was an art teacher. Young Pablo could draw with both his right and left hands before he even knew how to speak or write!

At age eight, he made his first painting, *The Little Yellow Picador*. It showed a *picador*—a bullfighter—on horseback. Pablo kept the painting for the rest of his life.

———

1881–1889

Student Life

Pablo studied painting in Barcelona, Spain, then in Madrid. He made many friends in both cities, meeting up with them in lively cafés.

In 1900, Pablo went to Paris, France, for the Exposition Universelle, a large art show. There he met art dealers who agreed to buy some of his paintings! It was his first taste of success.

A few years later Pablo moved to Paris. He would live there for many years.

———

1895–1900

Blue Period

Even though he sold some of his work, Pablo did not have much money. He struggled to make ends meet.

Pablo began painting sad pictures of sick and poor people, often using the color blue. He painted a blue picture of himself, too, called *Self-Portrait*.

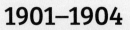

1901–1904

Rose Period

Around 1904, Pablo switched to more cheerful colors, especially pink. Some people think it was because he fell in love!

Pablo's most famous Rose Period painting was called *Les Demoiselles d'Avignon*, or *The Young Ladies of Avignon*. It was painted in a brand-new style that Pablo and his friend Georges Braque created. This style was called cubism.

___

1904–1907

Cubism

Most art at the time was realistic. Cubism was not. The people in cubist paintings looked as if they were made of cubes and triangles!

Pablo liked to add materials besides paint to his cubist works. Sometimes he glued bits of wood, sand, or newspaper onto the canvas.

Cubism shocked and thrilled the art world. Pablo's new paintings were displayed in important museums around the world. Pablo was famous!

———

1908–1915

Ballets Russes

On a trip to Rome, Italy, Pablo met Serge Diaghilev, the founder of a dance company called Ballets Russes, also known as The Russian Ballet. Serge asked Pablo to draw sets and costumes for his show.

While Pablo was working, he fell in love with one of the ballerinas, Olga Khokhlova. They got married on July 12, 1918. Three years later, they had a baby boy named Paulo.

—

1915–1925

Surrealism

Cubism had changed Pablo's career. Now Pablo decided to try another style: surrealism. He painted pictures with distorted shapes and people that were often disturbing. They could even look like nightmares!

At the same time, Pablo started making sculptures out of iron and stone. Some of them were very large. Pablo moved to a *château*, or a small castle, outside Paris called Boisgeloup. There he had enough space to work.

1925–1936

Pacifist

In 1936, civil war broke out in Pablo's home country, Spain. Pablo was shocked. He created a huge painting called *Guernica* that showed the horrors of war. The painting was presented at the Paris World's Fair in 1937.

Later, after World War II, Pablo painted a dove, symbolizing peace, for a World Peace Congress poster. The dove became popular around the world.

1936–1949

A New Life

Pablo moved to a small village in the South of France called Vallauris. The villagers there had a long tradition of making clay pottery.

Pablo began using clay to make art. In just a few years, he created thousands of pieces. He also continued to paint. He decorated a Vallauris chapel with a set of large paintings called *War and Peace*.

1948 — 1955

Last Years

Pablo spent his last days painting and sculpting in Vauvenargues, a château in France. On April 8, 1973, he died of heart failure. He was buried on the château grounds. Pablo Picasso made many masterpieces. He is one of the best-known and most important artists of all time.

———

1955–1973

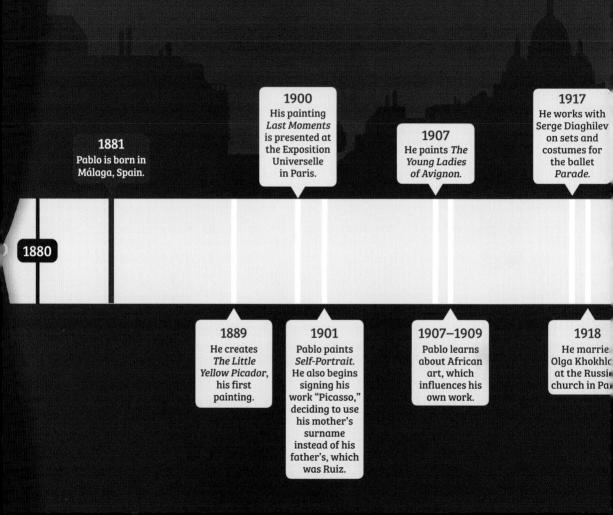

1881
Pablo is born in Málaga, Spain.

1900
His painting *Last Moments* is presented at the Exposition Universelle in Paris.

1907
He paints *The Young Ladies of Avignon*.

1917
He works with Serge Diaghilev on sets and costumes for the ballet *Parade*.

1880

1889
He creates *The Little Yellow Picador*, his first painting.

1901
Pablo paints *Self-Portrait*. He also begins signing his work "Picasso," deciding to use his mother's surname instead of his father's, which was Ruiz.

1907–1909
Pablo learns about African art, which influences his own work.

1918
He marrie Olga Khokhl at the Russi church in Pa

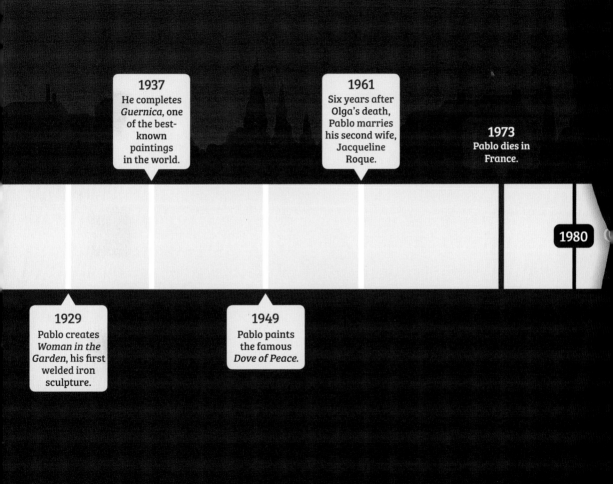

1937
He completes *Guernica*, one of the best-known paintings in the world.

1961
Six years after Olga's death, Pablo marries his second wife, Jacqueline Roque.

1973
Pablo dies in France.

1980

1929
Pablo creates *Woman in the Garden*, his first welded iron sculpture.

1949
Pablo paints the famous *Dove of Peace*.

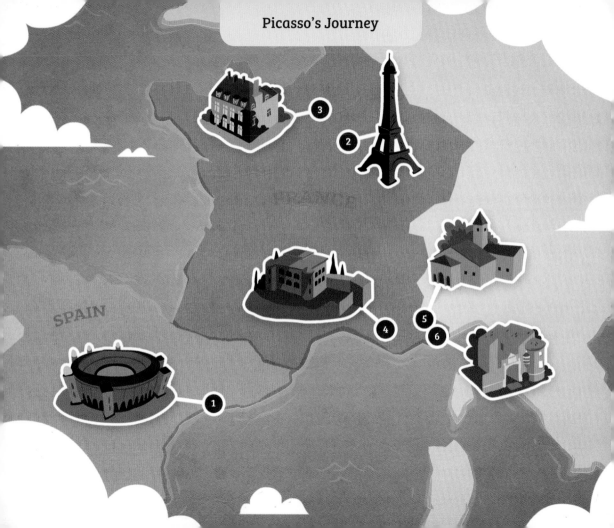

Picasso's Journey

MAP KEY

1 Barcelona, Spain

Pablo spent his youth in this capital city and had his first exhibition here. The Picasso Museum Barcelona celebrates Pablo's works from the years he lived in Spain—1890 to 1917.

2 Paris, France

Pablo spent many years in Paris and often changed studios. There's a museum dedicated to Pablo at the Hôtel Salé.

3 Château de Boisgeloup, France

This castle, where Pablo lived from 1930 to 1935, is located forty miles from Paris. He sculpted and painted and received guests here.

4 Château de Vauvenargues, France

Pablo bought this castle in 1958. It was built in the eighteenth century at the foot of Sainte-Victoire Mountain. Pablo is buried here with Jacqueline.

5 Mougins, France

Pablo and Jacqueline settled in this small French Riviera town in 1961.

6 Vallauris, France

Pablo discovered this village of potters in 1948. He painted *War and Peace* on the walls of the chapel here, which is now the Picasso National Museum.

People to Know

Max Jacob
(1876–1944)
Pablo befriended many artists and writers in
Paris, including this poet.

Jean Cocteau
(1889–1963)
Pablo's closest friend was the writer Jean
Cocteau. Jean introduced Pablo to Serge
Diaghilev of Ballets Russes.

Guillaume Apollinaire
(1880–1918)
This writer was another of Pablo's good friends. Max and Guillaume were witnesses at Pablo's wedding to Olga.

Brassaï
(1899–1984)
This Hungarian journalist met Pablo in 1932. He photographed the artist at home and at work for more than ten years, leaving an extraordinary record of Pablo's life.

Pablo was baptized with a long string of names: Pablo Diego José Francisco de Paula Juan Nepomuceno Crispín Crispiniano María de los Remedios de la Santísima Trinidad Ruiz Picasso.

At the time of his death, Pablo was ninety-one years old. It's estimated that he created fifty thousand pieces of art during his lifetime.

During World War II, Pablo stayed in Paris while the Germans occupied the city. A German officer searched Pablo's apartment and saw a photograph of his Guernica painting. "Did you do that?" asked the officer. "No," Pablo replied. "You did."

More of Pablo's paintings have been stolen than any other artist's. In 2012, the Art Loss Register listed 1,147 of his works as stolen.

Available Now